Elliott Michaelson
MAJS

Copyright Information

PARASHAT BERESHIT

Vital Statistics	
Full text reference:	*Genesis / Bereshit 1: 1 to 6: 8*
First Aliyah:	*Genesis / Bereshit 1: 1 to 1: 5*
Second Aliyah:	*Genesis / Bereshit 1: 6 to 1: 8*
Third Aliyah:	*Genesis / Bereshit 1: 9 to 1: 13*

Note: the English retelling of the Torah is for the entire *parashah*, not just the Shabbat pm / Weekday readings. The English for these readings consists of the first part of the retelling.

MY PROGRESS

Date	Torah blessings	Torah reading	Torah review in English

Date	*Torah blessings*	*Torah reading*	*Torah review in English*

Date	*Torah blessings*	*Torah reading*	*Torah review in English*

Date	Torah blessings	Torah reading	Torah review in English

BEFORE YOU BEGIN: GOOD THINGS TO ASK ABOUT THIS BOOK

Welcome to your Bar/Bat Mitzvah Survival Guide! There are some unique features about this guide that might be useful to you during your studies, such as...

What's up with the names of people and places?

Brace yourself, for what I'm about to say (or write, actually) may come as a shock. THE TORAH IS WRITTEN IN HEBREW. Big surprise, I know. So here's the issue many of my students have: in English, we call him *Moses* but in the Torah, we call him *Moshe*. The first woman on Earth is called *Eve* but in Hebrew, she's called *Hava*. The Jews were slaves in *Egypt* — or was it *Mitzra'im*? The answer is both. To try to avoid this confusion between English and Hebrew names, I've decided to stick with the Hebrew. So מֹשֶׁה is translated as *Moshe*, not *Moses*, and יְרוּשָׁלַיִם is *Yerushalayim*, not *Jerusalem*. For more on how to pronounce the Hebrew names, check out the handy translation chart on page ten.

How do you show God talking?

Many of us think of God as an inspirational force in our lives, but how many of us have actual physical conversations with God? As a kid, I was always confused by the fact that God physically speaks to people in the Torah but not to us today. When the Torah records God's "speech", we don't have to think of it as physical words all the time. Moses Maimonides was one of the greatest philosophers and teachers in Judaism, and 800 years ago he famously taught that all divine language in the Torah is metaphorical. Taking that to heart, I've done my very best to express that in my English retellings. God's "dialogue" is written in a different font and with a different tone, and I avoid using direct language like "said" or "told". So did Avraham hear the actual voice of God, or did God act as Avraham's inspirational inner voice? Both beliefs are valid, and it's something I encourage you to explore with your family and your teacher / rabbi.

In these retellings, I refer to God by two proper nouns: *Adonai* and *Elohim*. *Adonai* is God's actual, personal name: י-ה-ו-ה. You'll find it all over the place in the Tanah and in many sidurim. *Elohim* (אֱלֹהִים) is the Hebrew word for "God". Since the Tanah uses both as personal names for God, I've decided to keep the proper Hebrew terms.

What about commentary and translation?

Judaism has always accepted that the Torah text contains four layers of understanding. There's the literal, basic text that you see in front of you (peshat), but underneath the basic text are three layers of metaphorical understanding just waiting to be discovered (derash, remez, sod). You have over two thousand years of scholarship and commentary — including some great stuff being written today — to help you discover these hidden meanings. I've deliberately avoided providing them here for one all-important reason: any commentaries I select would reflect *my* perspective on the text and how it should be taught, and I want you to be free to find *your own way*. That's why I'm leaving the selection of commentary up to you and your rabbi / teacher.

Instead, I've devoted my time to a careful retelling of the Torah and Haftarah texts in English. This isn't a strict translation, but it isn't a sanitized children's version, either. My aim is to provide an English format that flows as easily as a work of juvenile literature, but which preserves the content and significance of the Biblical text. I've also included suggestions for study and analysis that are based on media literacy expectations from public school programs. These blurbs usually address social and historical questions that my own students ask because they need help understanding the ancient society that produced our sacred texts. None of this replaces Rabbinic commentary, but first you need to understand a little bit about the world of our ancient cousins. Then you can work with your rabbi / teacher to find the commentaries that speak to your own interests and concerns.

Da Links!

If you're using the ebook version of this book, try tapping the hyperlinks that appear periodically in the text. Some of them will take you to useful Google maps of many of the locations mentioned in the Torah, while others will take you the *Jewish Virtual Library* or *My Jewish Learning* to learn more about the famous people and nations from the Torah and Haftarah. Enjoy!

-- EM, fall 2015

TRANSLITERATIONS OF HEBREW VOWEL SOUNDS

(A very handy reference guide...)

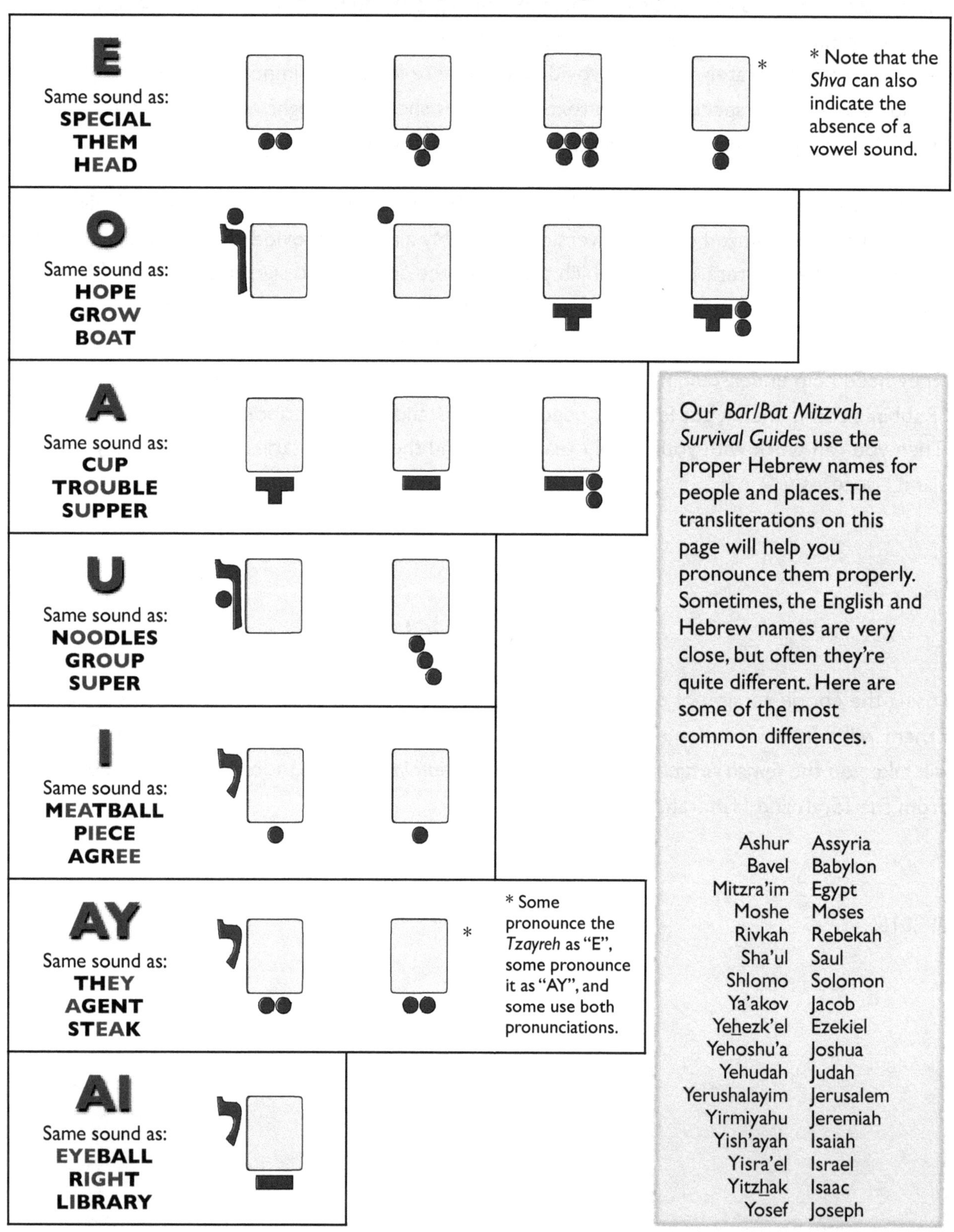

Our *Bar/Bat Mitzvah Survival Guides* use the proper Hebrew names for people and places. The transliterations on this page will help you pronounce them properly. Sometimes, the English and Hebrew names are very close, but often they're quite different. Here are some of the most common differences.

Ashur	Assyria
Bavel	Babylon
Mitzra'im	Egypt
Moshe	Moses
Rivkah	Rebekah
Sha'ul	Saul
Shlomo	Solomon
Ya'akov	Jacob
Yehezk'el	Ezekiel
Yehoshu'a	Joshua
Yehudah	Judah
Yerushalayim	Jerusalem
Yirmiyahu	Jeremiah
Yish'ayah	Isaiah
Yisra'el	Israel
Yitzhak	Isaac
Yosef	Joseph

PUTTING ON THE TALLIT & TEFILLIN

If you've never had the chance to put on the *tallit* or *tefillin*, this is your lucky day! Traditionally, the *tallit* and *tefillin* are worn for all weekday morning services. On Shabbat and Holy Day mornings, only the *tallit* is worn (except Yom Kippur, when we wear the tallit all day). Why the difference? There are many explanations. My favorite reason goes like this: the Torah teaches us to wear reminders of our Divine Agreement with God on our arms and our heads (i.e. *tefillin)*. On Shabbat, Pesah̲, Shavu'ot, Sukkot, Rosh Hashanah, and Yom Kippur, we perform rituals all day long that remind us of God's Agreement with us, so we don't need the *tefillin* to remind us. To put everything on, follow these basic steps. You can also find a video on our website at **http://www.adventurejudaism.net/Bar_Bat_Mitzvah_Guides.html**.

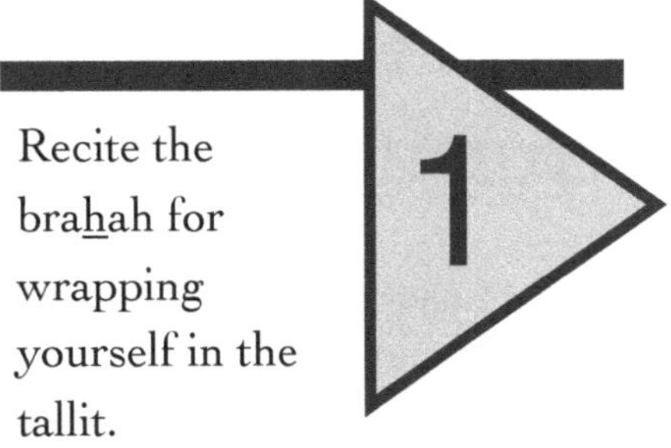

בָּרוּךְ אַתָּה יְיָ אֱלֹהֵינוּ מֶלֶךְ הָעוֹלָם, אֲשֶׁר
קִדְּשָׁנוּ בְּמִצְוֹתָיו, וְצִוָּנוּ לְהִתְעַטֵּף בַּצִּיצִת.

We praise You, Adonai our God, Ruler of the universe, whose *mitzvot* make us holy, and who commanded us to cover ourselves with *tzitzit*.

On Shabbat and Holy Day mornings, stop here!

Loop the *tefillin shel yad* (the one with the extra-long strap) around your bicep.

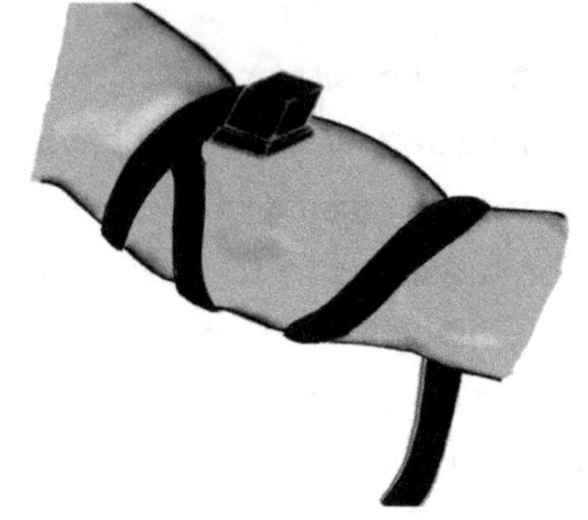

If you're left-handed, use your right bicep. If you're right-handed, use your left bicep. If you're ambidextrous like me, take your pick!

Before tightening the loop, recite this bra<u>h</u>ah.

בָּרוּךְ אַתָּה יְיָ אֱלֹהֵינוּ מֶלֶךְ הָעוֹלָם, אֲשֶׁר
קִדְּשָׁנוּ בְּמִצְוֹתָיו, וְצִוָּנוּ לְהָנִיחַ תְּפִלִּין.

We praise You, Adonai our God, Ruler of the universe, whose *mitzvot* make us holy, and who commanded us to put on *tefillin*.

Tighten the loop around your bicep and wrap the strap around your forearm 7 times.

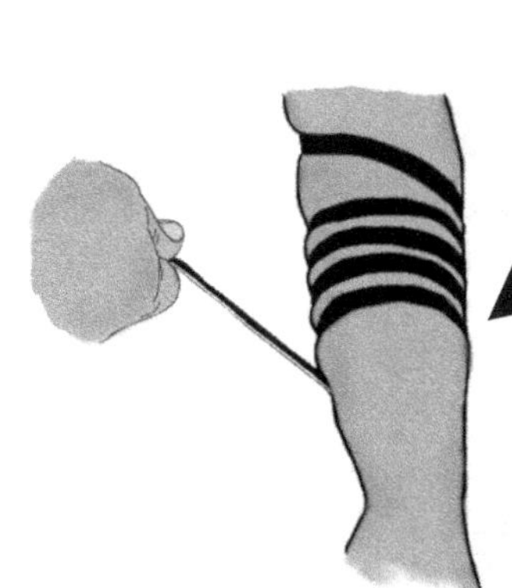

Wrap the strap around your forearm 7 times.

If the strap is long enough, use the extra length to keep the *tefillin* box in place on your bicep.

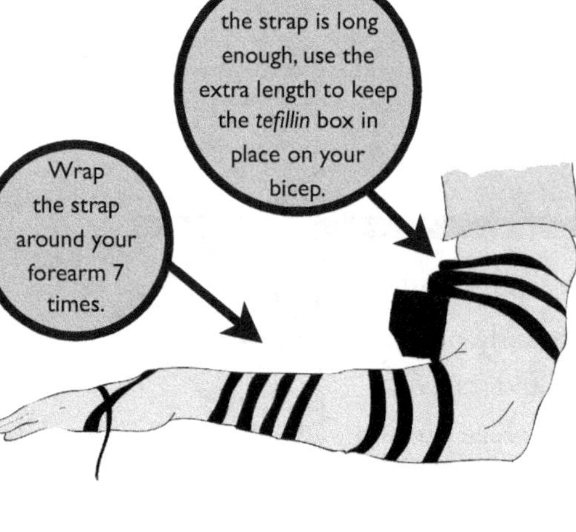

Place the *tefillin shel rosh* at the center of your forehead, right at the hairline.

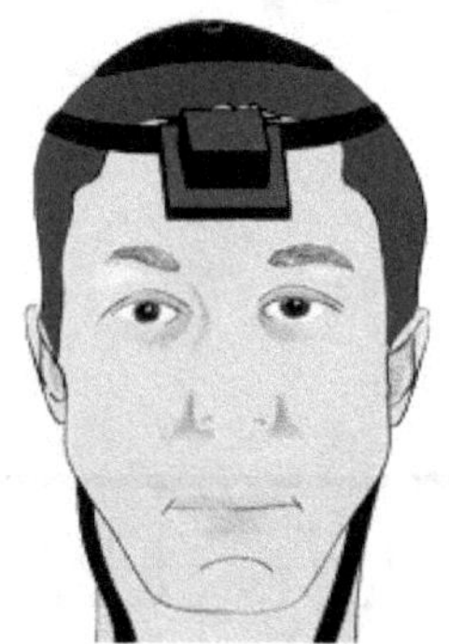

Two long straps extend from the back of the *tefillin shel rosh*. Let them hang freely on either side of your head.

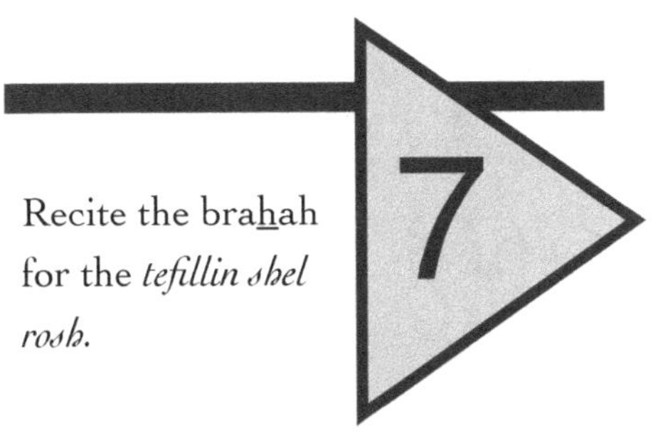

Recite the brahah for the *tefillin shel rosh.*

בָּרוּךְ אַתָּה יְיָ אֱלֹהֵינוּ מֶלֶךְ הָעוֹלָם, אֲשֶׁר קִדְּשָׁנוּ בְּמִצְוֹתָיו, וְצִוָּנוּ עַל מִצְוַת תְּפִלִּין.

We praise You, Adonai our God, Ruler of the universe, whose *mitzvot* make us holy, and who commanded the *mitzvah* of *tefillin*.

Finish wrapping the *tefillin shel yad* by winding it around your middle finger 3 times.

If the strap is long enough, you can also wind it around your hand to help keep everything in place.

You're ready to go! When you're finished, take everything off in the reverse order.

THE TORAH IN ENGLISH

BERESHIT / GENESIS 1: 1 TO 6: 8

What's the story so far?

Okay, you got me. How can there be a "story so far" if this is the first parashah in the Torah? Good question. One answer is that the Torah has no start or finish. We read it in a cycle, so that when we reach the last parashah we immediately rewind and start again with the first parashah. Since we read the whole Torah every year, when we read *Bereshit*, we make connections to what we know happens later on. For example, when we read about the separation of Shabbat as a day of rest at the end of Creation, the Torah expects us to connect this to mitzvot in later books that outline the observance of Shabbat. When we read about the laws of Shabbat later on (say, in the Ten Commandments), we're expected to make connections to events in *Bereshit*.

What can I expect from this parashah?

There's a lot going on in *Bereshit*. God creates everything (twice); the first human beings are placed in Eden; they eat from the forbidden tree and are severely punished & exiled; one of their sons kills the other following a mysterious argument; humanity spreads out across the earth and fills the world with corruption. The parashah ends ominously with God regretting the act of Creation.

Much of *Bereshit* is hard to accept at face value, and people who treat the Torah like a science textbook are going to be disappointed. You won't find any support for scientific theories like Big Bang, Evolution, or Natural Selection to explain how the world came to be and how life began. That's because Science is about human inspiration and observation, but Torah study is about divine inspiration. In other words, Science tells us how the universe works; Torah teaches us what the universe's workings mean for us as human beings. Keep this in mind as you read through the parashah.

And so, without further ado, on to the Torah...

Creation

1: 1-5
The Shabbat pm /
Weekday Torah
reading starts here.

When Elohim began creating the heavens and the earth, the earth had no shape or form, and everything was in darkness and chaos.
Elohim's spirit swept over the water.

Let there be light!

There was light. Elohim saw that this was good. Elohim separated Light from Darkness to make the first Day and Night.

Evening and morning passed for the First Day.

When Elohim began creating: How can the Torah say that the world was created in six days when everything we know about science says otherwise? The Torah is a book of *religion*, not *science*. Science explains how the universe works. Religion teaches us what the universe's workings *mean* to us as human beings. Think of it this way: your science textbook uses theories like Evolution and Natural Selection to explain how human beings came to exist as we are today. The Torah (and 3000 years of prophets and rabbis) teaches us about the moral and ethical responsibilities that come with being human. As you read through the rest of *Bereshit*, think about the difference between religion and science. Think *metaphorically*, not *literally*.

1: 6-8

Let there be a division to separate the water!

It happened. Elohim separated the water, placing some of it above the division and some of it below. Elohim called the division "Sky". Evening and morning passed for the Second Day.

1: 9-13
The Shabbat pm /
Weekday Torah
reading ends at vs. 13.

Let the water under the sky be gathered into one place so that dry areas can be seen!

It happened. Elohim called the dry areas "Land", and the areas with water Elohim called "Seas". Elohim saw that this was good.

Let the land grow mature plant life with ripe seeds and fruit!

It happened. The land grew mature plants of every kind. Seeing this, Elohim felt good. Evening and morning passed for the Third Day.

1: 14-19

Let there be lights in the Sky to distinguish between Day and Night, and to allow festivals, days, and years to be marked off. Let these lights illuminate the Land!

It happened. Elohim assembled the two largest lights: the greater one to illuminate Day and the smaller one to illuminate Night, along with the stars. Elohim placed them in the Sky to provide light for the Land and to separate Day and Night.

Elohim saw that this was good. Evening and morning passed for the Fourth Day.

1: 20-23

Let the Sea fill with animal life, and let the Land fill with birds that fly across the Sky!

Elohim created the largest sea creatures and all the other species of animal life that fill the Sea, along with every species of bird. Elohim saw that this was good, and blessed them.

Be fruitful, have many offspring, and fill the Sea and the Land!

Evening and morning passed for the Fifth Day.

1: 24-28

Let the Land produce every species of roaming animal, insect, and everything that crawls on the ground.

It happened. Elohim made every species of roaming animal, insect, and everything that crawls. Elohim saw that this was good.

Let Us make Humans in Our image, to be like Us. They will take charge of the animals in the Sea, the birds of the Sky, and all the creatures that live on the Land.

Elohim created Humans in Elohim's image, and made male and female together. Elohim blessed them.

1: 28-31

> **Elohim created humans...:** Human beings are arguably the most powerful creatures on Earth (at least, we like to think we are). So why do you think the Torah says that we were created last — shouldn't we have come first? If everything was here before we were, what might this say about our role in the world? How does this affect your understanding of God's blessing in the next paragraph?
>
> And what's this about being created in God's image? God has no physical shape. How can you be created in the image of something that has no shape? Hint: the word "image" has more than one meaning. Keep this metaphor in mind as you continue reading the Eden story...

Be fruitful, have many offspring, fill the Land, and be in command over it. Take charge of the animals in the Sea, the birds of the Sky, and all the creatures that live on the Land. For food, I give you the grasses of the field and the fruit trees. To the birds of the Sky and the creatures on the Land, I give all forms of vegetation to eat.

Elohim saw everything that had been accomplished, and it was very good. Evening and morning passed for the Sixth Day.

Eden

2: 1-3

The creation of heaven, earth, and everything in them was now complete. By the Seventh Day, all the labor was done, and Elohim rested from the effort. Since this was the day of rest from all the creative work that Elohim set out to do, Elohim blessed the Seventh Day and made it holy.

2: 4-9

HERE IS THE ***HISTORY OF THE CREATION OF HEAVEN AND EARTH*** *ON THE DAY THEY WERE MADE BY ADONAI ELOHIM...*

> **History of the creation of heaven and earth:** Here we see a second Creation story. How does this one compare with the previous one? Remember that the Torah is a book of *religion*, not *science*. Explore the moral lessons embedded in this story. Remember: think metaphorically!

There wasn't any vegetation on the land because Adonai hadn't yet caused the rain to fall, nor was there any human to till the soil. There was only a mist that welled out of the earth to moisten the ground. Adonai Elohim molded a man out of the dust on the ground, breathed a soul into his nostrils, and brought him to life. Adonai Elohim planted a garden in Eden — in the East — and put the man there. Adonai Elohim caused all kinds of trees to grow that are good for eating, along with the Tree of Life and the Tree of Knowledge of Good and Evil.

2: 10-14

A stream flows out of Eden to water the garden, and it splits into the headwaters of four rivers. The first is called Pishon, and it winds around the land of Havilah where the gold is (the gold there is of good quality, and so are the bdellium and lapis-lazuli.) The second river is called Gihon, and it winds around the land of Cush. The third river is called Hidekel, and it runs east of **Ashur**. The fourth river is called **Ferat**.

Ashur: This is the ancient kingdom of Assyria.

Ferat: The name "Ferat" is Hebrew for the Euphrates, which flows through modern-day Iraq and Syria.

2: 15-25

Adonai Elohim put the man in the garden of Eden to till it and to protect it.

You will eat from any tree in this garden ***except the Tree of Knowledge of Good and Evil.***
On the day you eat from that tree, YOU WILL DIE.

Adonai Elohim considered the man.

It is not proper for the man to be alone. I will make a counterpart for him to help him.

Adonai Elohim molded from the ground all the animals of the field and the birds of the sky, and brought them to the man to see what the man would call them. Whatever the man called them would be their name. The man gave names to all the animals and the birds, but he didn't find a counterpart to help him. So Adonai Elohim put the man into a deep sleep. While the man slept, Adonai Elohim removed one of his ribs and sealed the wound. Adonai Elohim used the rib to make a woman and brought her to the man.

Tree of Knowledge...: Think about what you know about how people behave. Why *wouldn't* God want humanity to know about Good and Evil? Explore the consequences of having this knowledge?

When the man saw her, he announced, "Finally, someone who's the bone from my bones and the flesh from my flesh! I will call her **'Woman' since she was taken from 'Man'.**"

This is why a man leaves his father and mother to bond with his wife — as if they're one flesh.

The man and his woman were naked, but they weren't ashamed about it.

'Woman'...: This is a pun on the Hebrew words for man (אִישׁ) and woman (אִשָּׁה).

EXILE FROM PARADISE

3: 1-7

Of all the animals created by Adonai Elohim, the snake was the most mischievous. "Did Elohim really tell you not to eat from any tree in the garden?" he asked the woman.

"No, we can eat from any fruit tree in the garden," she replied. "It was only the tree in the center of the garden that Elohim told us not to eat from. We can't even to touch it or we'll die."

"You *won't* die," argued the snake. "Elohim knows that the moment you eat from it, your inner awareness will open and you'll be like Elohim – knowing Good from Evil."

The woman gazed longingly at the tree. She saw that the fruit looked very delicious and that it would make her wise, so she took one and ate it. Then she gave one to her husband and he ate it, too. Suddenly, their inner awareness opened and they realized that they were naked. Sewing together some fig leaves, they made crude underwear.

3:8-19

As evening came, they felt Adonai Elohim's presence blowing through the garden. The man and woman hid themselves among the trees.

Where are you?

"We felt Your Presence in the garden," stammered the man. "We realized we were naked, so we hid."

Who said you that you were naked? You have eaten from the tree, have you not — the one I told you not to eat from!

The man trembled. "It was the woman You created to be with me! She brought me the fruit and I ate it!"

The woman felt Adonai Elohim's presence directed at her.

What have you done?

"It was the snake," cried the woman. "He tricked me into eating it!"

> Okay, so the man and the woman had one simple rule to follow, and they couldn't even manage to do that. Joking aside, consider the lesson here. What is the Torah trying to teach us about human behavior? How does this event compare to other moments of disobedience and punishment later on in the Torah? Explore your ideas!

Because you did this, Snake, you will be cursed among all living things. You are doomed to crawl on your belly and eat dirt for all the days of your life. There will be hatred between you and the woman, and between your descendants and hers. They will strike at your head, and you will strike at their heel.

As for you, Woman, the labors of childbirth will be multiplied, and you will give birth in great pain. You will long for your man, and he will dominate you.

And you, Man: you listened to your wife when she gave you the fruit to eat — after I commanded you not to eat from the tree! The ground will be cursed because of you. Only through hard labor will you benefit from it, though it will produce weeds and thorns, and you will eat only from the grasses of the field. Only by the sweat of your brow will you have bread to eat until the day you return to the earth. You are dust, and to dust you will return!

3: 20-23

The man named his wife **Hava because she was the mother of all living things**, and Adonai Elohim provided clothes for them made from animal skins.

> **Hava...:** In Hebrew, her name is חַוָּה, which is usually translated as "Eve". חַוָּה is related to the word חַי, which means "life".

By knowing Good and Evil, humans have now become like one of Us. They have only to stretch out a hand to the Tree of Life and eat the fruit. Then they will live forever!

Adonai Elohim exiled the humans from the garden of Eden, where the man now had to till the ground from which he was taken. Having banished them, Adonai Elohim set the **Keruvim** and a spinning, flaming sword to guard the garden of Eden — and the way to the Tree of Life — from the East.

> **Keruvim:** These were mythical winged creatures with human and animal features. The Tanah (Jewish Bible) isn't entirely clear as to exactly what Keruvim looked like, but our ancestors certainly knew. During the time of Moshe (Moses), the top of the Aron (the chest where the first mitzvot were kept) was decorated with two golden Keruvim.

First Kill

The story of humanity's first kill has troubled readers for thousands of years. Like the rest of the events in this parashah, reflect on this metaphorically, not just literally. What moral lessons are embedded here?

4: 1-7

The man slept with his wife, Hava. She became pregnant and gave birth to **Kayin**. Explaining the meaning of his name, she said, "I have gotten a man from Adonai." She then gave birth to his brother, **Hevel**. Hevel became a shepherd while Kayin became a farmer.

Time passed. Kayin brought an offering to Adonai from his crops, and Hevel brought the best of his flock's first-born. Adonai acknowledged Hevel and his offering, but Adonai did not acknowledge Kayin and his offering. Kayin turned away in rage.

Kayin: In Hebrew, קַיִן is connected to the phrase "I have gotten" (קָנִיתִי).

Hevel: In Hebrew, הֶבֶל means "breath" or "vapor", though the Torah doesn't provide a reason for his name.

Why are you furious, and why hide your face? Surely, if you do Good, you will be uplifted. But if you do not, evil deeds will lurk at the door. You will feel their urges, but you can master them.

4: 8-15

Kayin spoke to his brother, Hevel. When they were out in the field, Kayin attacked his brother and killed him.

Where is your brother Hevel?

Responding to Adonai's Presence, Kayin answered, "I don't know. Am I my brother's guardian?"

What have you done? Your brother's blood cries out to Me from the ground! You are cursed from the ground, which opened its mouth to take your brother's blood from your hands! When you farm the land, it will no longer give its crop to you. You shall wander the earth forever!

Distraught, Kayin cried out to Adonai, "My punishment is too severe! You've exiled me from the land, and I'll have to hide myself from You. As a wanderer, anyone who sees me might kill me!"

My vengeance shall be seven times greater on whomever kills Kayin!

Adonai placed a mark on Kayin as a warning about the curse to anyone who might attack him.

4: 16-24

Kayin left Adonai's Presence and settled in the land of Nod, which is east of Eden. He slept with his wife, she became pregnant, and gave birth to H̲anoh̲. Kayin built a city and named it after his son. When H̲anoh̲ grew up, he had a son named Irad. Irad had a son named Meh̲uya'el, who in turn had a son named Metusha'el. Metusha'el's son was Lameh̲.

Lameh̲ had two wives: Adah and Tzillah. Adah gave birth to Yavval, who is the ancestor of people who live among their herds in tents. His brother's name was Yuvval, and he is the ancestor of musicians who play the lyre and the pipe. Tzillah also had children. She gave birth to Tuvval-Kayin, who made all kinds of copper and iron tools. Tuvval-Kayin's sister was Na'amah.

One day, **Lameh̲ announced to his wives**: "Listen to what I have to say! I killed a man who wounded me and a boy who bruised me. If the vengeance on Kayin is seven times greater, mine will be seventy-seven!"

Lameh̲ announced...: What does this mini-story have to do with the main story of Adam and H̲ava? Not much. The Torah has several mini-stories like this that don't seem to go anywhere. At one time, many centuries ago, this story may have been complete. Who knows how many other ancient Jewish traditions have been lost to time...?

4: 25-26

Adam slept with his wife again. She had a son and called him **Shet**. She explained the meaning of his name: "Elohim has provided me with another child in place of Hevel, who was killed by Kayin." When Shet grew up, he had a son of his own named Enosh. It was at that time when people began to pray to Adonai by name.

Adam: The Hebrew name אָדָם means "human". The word הָאָדָם means "the man". The end of Chapter 4 is the first time when the Torah uses אָדָם as a proper name.

Shet: The Hebrew שֵׁת is connected to the phrase "provided me with..." (שָׁת-לִי).

Filling The Land

5: 1-20

THIS IS THE BOOK OF THE HISTORY OF HUMANITY...

On the day they were created by Elohim, they were made in Elohim's image — male and female. Elohim blessed them and called them "humans". When Adam was 130 years old, he had a son in his own image named Shet. After Shet was born, Adam lived for another 800 years, and he had more sons and daughters in that time. Adam died at the age of 930.

What's the point of this exhaustive family tree? The Torah isn't only concerned with teaching us about positive behavior and religion. It's also concerned about teaching us history. Not *scientific* history with archeologists and old relics, but the memory of *oral* history. Our ancient cousins were very interested in remembering where they came from and how different people came to be. Preserving this knowledge was very important to them. Why might this be? How do we benefit today from knowing our family histories? Discuss your ideas!

When Shet was 105, he had a son named Enosh. Shet lived for another 807 years, and he had more sons and daughters. Shet died at the age of 912. When Enosh was 90, he had Kaynan. Enosh lived for another 815 years, and he had more sons and daughters. Enosh died at the age of 905. When Kaynan was 70, he had Mahalal'el. Kaynan lived for another 840 years, had more sons and daughters, and died at the age of 910. Mahalal'el was 65 years old when he had Yared. Mahalal'el lived for another 830 years, had more sons and daughters, and died at the age of 895. When Yared was 162 years old, he had Hanoh. Yared lived another 800 years, had more sons and daughters, and died at the age of 962.

5: 21-32

When Hanoh was 65 years old, he had Metushalah. After Metushalah's birth, Hanoh walked with Elohim for 300 years, and had more sons and daughters. Hanoh lived for 365 years. He walked with Elohim, but he disappeared — for Elohim took him.

When Metushalah was 187, he had Lameh. Metushalah lived for another 782 years, had more sons and daughters, and died at the age of 969.

When Lameh was 182, he had a son whom he named No'ah. Lameh explained No'ah's name: "This child will give us relief from our hard work and manual labor on the ground that Adonai cursed." Lameh lived for another 595 years and had more sons and daughters. He died at the age of 777.

No'ah: The Hebrew נֹחַ is connected to the phrase "will give us relief / comfort" (יְנַחֲמֵנוּ).

When No'ah was 500 years old, he had Shem, Ham, and Yafet.

Elohim's Regret

6: 1-4

When the human population increased across the earth, they had many daughters. Elohim's divine followers saw how beautiful they were, and they took any of the daughters they wanted to be their wives.

My breath will not last in humanity forever, for they are made of flesh. Let their lifespan be 120 years!

Elohim's divine followers had children with humanity's daughters. These children were called "Nefilim". These were the heroes of ancient legend.

6: 5-8
This is the Maftir.

Adonai witnessed humanity's great evil in the world. Every desire in their hearts was always wicked. With great sorrow, Adonai regretted making humans.

Adonai witnessed humanity's great evil...: What a great cliffhanger! Cue the ominous music. Of course, our ancient cousins who first read this (or heard it) already knew what comes next, and so should we. But apart from the desire for a good ending, what might the earliest rabbis be trying to teach us by closing the parashah here? Explore the connection between God's decisions here and in the garden of Eden.

I shall wipe out the humans I have made from the face of the earth and every living creature with them.

Only No'ah was acceptable to Adonai.

Up next...

No'ah! God approaches the only righteous man in this horrid generation worth saving: No'ah. The scheme to wipe out and restart all life on earth is hatched as No'ah builds an enormous boat to save two of every species from destruction. When it's all over, God makes a commitment to never again wipe out all life... At least, not with a flood. No'ah's sons have many descendants, and apart from a few slip-ups (notably, a certain babbling tower), manage to thrive. The parashah ends by zeroing in on one of No'ah's descendants — a rather famous individual whom God chooses to be the father of a great nation.

THE TORAH IN HEBREW
BLESSINGS & READINGS (BERESHIT 1: 1-13)

Before the Torah reading, recite one of the following blessings.
Your Rabbi or teacher will tell you which one is appropriate for your community.

You call out:

בָּרְכוּ אֶת יְיָ הַמְבֹרָךְ.

The congregation responds:

בָּרוּךְ יְיָ הַמְבֹרָךְ לְעוֹלָם וָעֶד.

You say it back to them:

בָּרוּךְ יְיָ הַמְבֹרָךְ לְעוֹלָם וָעֶד.

You continue:

בָּרוּךְ אַתָּה יְיָ אֱלֹהֵינוּ מֶלֶךְ הָעוֹלָם,

אֲשֶׁר קֵרְבָנוּ לַעֲבוֹדָתוֹ

וְנָתַן לָנוּ אֶת תּוֹרָתוֹ.

בָּרוּךְ אַתָּה יְיָ, נוֹתֵן הַתּוֹרָה.

Let us praise Adonai,
the Blessed One!

Let Adonai, the Blessed One,
be praised forever!

We praise You, Adonai our God,
Ruler of the universe,
Who drew us close to God's Work
and gave us God's Torah.

We praise You, Adonai,
the Giver of Torah.

You call out:

בָּרְכוּ אֶת יְיָ הַמְבֹרָךְ.

The congregation responds:

בָּרוּךְ יְיָ הַמְבֹרָךְ לְעוֹלָם וָעֶד.

You say it back to them:

בָּרוּךְ יְיָ הַמְבֹרָךְ לְעוֹלָם וָעֶד.

You continue:

בָּרוּךְ אַתָּה יְיָ אֱלֹהֵינוּ מֶלֶךְ הָעוֹלָם,

אֲשֶׁר בָּחַר בָּנוּ מִכָּל הָעַמִּים

וְנָתַן לָנוּ אֶת תּוֹרָתוֹ.

בָּרוּךְ אַתָּה יְיָ, נוֹתֵן הַתּוֹרָה.

Let us praise Adonai,
the Blessed One!

Let Adonai, the Blessed One,
be praised forever!

We praise You, Adonai our God,
Ruler of the universe,
Who chose us from all the nations
to be given God's Torah.

We praise You, Adonai,
the Giver of Torah.

בראשית ברא אלהים את השמים
ואת הארץ והארץ היתה תהו ובהו
וחשך על פני תהום ורוח אלהים
מרחפת על פני המים ויאמר אלהים
יהי אור ויהי אור וירא אלהים את
האור כי טוב ויבדל אלהים בין
האור ובין החשך ויקרא אלהים
לאור יום ולחשך קרא לילה ויהי
ערב ויהי בקר יום אחד

ויאמר אלהים יהי רקיע בתוך המים
ויהי מבדיל בין מים למים ויעש
אלהים את הרקיע ויבדל בין המים
אשר מתחת לרקיע ובין המים אשר
מעל לרקיע ויהי כן ויקרא אלהים
לרקיע שמים ויהי ערב ויהי בקר יום
שני

עליה א׳

1. בְּרֵאשִׁ֖ית בָּרָ֣א אֱלֹהִ֑ים
אֵ֥ת הַשָּׁמַ֖יִם וְאֵ֥ת הָאָֽרֶץ׃

2. וְהָאָ֗רֶץ
הָיְתָ֥ה תֹ֙הוּ֙ וָבֹ֔הוּ
וְחֹ֖שֶׁךְ עַל־פְּנֵ֣י תְה֑וֹם
וְר֣וּחַ אֱלֹהִ֔ים
מְרַחֶ֖פֶת עַל־פְּנֵ֥י הַמָּֽיִם׃

3. וַיֹּ֥אמֶר אֱלֹהִ֖ים יְהִ֣י־א֑וֹר
וַֽיְהִי־אֽוֹר׃

4. וַיַּ֧רְא אֱלֹהִ֛ים
אֶת־הָא֖וֹר כִּי־ט֑וֹב
וַיַּבְדֵּ֣ל אֱלֹהִ֔ים
בֵּ֥ין הָא֖וֹר וּבֵ֥ין הַחֹֽשֶׁךְ׃

5. וַיִּקְרָ֨א אֱלֹהִ֤ים ׀ לָאוֹר֙ י֔וֹם
וְלַחֹ֖שֶׁךְ קָ֣רָא לָ֑יְלָה
וַֽיְהִי־עֶ֥רֶב וַֽיְהִי־בֹ֖קֶר י֥וֹם אֶחָֽד׃

עליה ב׳

6. וַיֹּ֣אמֶר אֱלֹהִ֔ים
יְהִ֥י רָקִ֖יעַ בְּת֣וֹךְ הַמָּ֑יִם
וִיהִ֣י מַבְדִּ֔יל
בֵּ֥ין מַ֖יִם לָמָֽיִם׃

7. וַיַּ֣עַשׂ אֱלֹהִים֮ אֶת־הָרָקִיעַ֒
וַיַּבְדֵּ֗ל
בֵּ֤ין הַמַּ֙יִם֙ אֲשֶׁר֙ מִתַּ֣חַת לָרָקִ֔יעַ
וּבֵ֥ין הַמַּ֖יִם
אֲשֶׁ֣ר מֵעַ֣ל לָרָקִ֑יעַ
וַֽיְהִי־כֵֽן׃

8. וַיִּקְרָ֧א אֱלֹהִ֛ים
לָֽרָקִ֖יעַ שָׁמָ֑יִם
וַֽיְהִי־עֶ֥רֶב וַֽיְהִי־בֹ֖קֶר י֥וֹם שֵׁנִֽי׃

12. וַתּוֹצֵ֨א הָאָ֜רֶץ
דֶּ֠שֶׁא
עֵ֣שֶׂב מַזְרִ֤יעַ זֶ֙רַע֙ לְמִינֵ֔הוּ
וְעֵ֧ץ עֹֽשֶׂה־פְּרִ֛י
אֲשֶׁ֥ר זַרְעוֹ־ב֖וֹ לְמִינֵ֑הוּ
וַיַּ֥רְא אֱלֹהִ֖ים כִּי־טֽוֹב׃

13. וַֽיְהִי־עֶ֥רֶב וַֽיְהִי־בֹ֖קֶר
י֥וֹם שְׁלִישִֽׁי׃

ויאמר אלהים יקוו המים מתחת
השמים אל מקום אחד ותראה
היבשה ויהי כן ויקרא אלהים
ליבשה ארץ ולמקוה המים קרא
ימים וירא אלהים כי טוב ויאמר
אלהים תדשא הארץ דשא עשב
מזריע זרע עץ פרי עשה פרי למינו
אשר זרעו בו על הארץ ויהי
כן ותוצא הארץ דשא עשב מזריע
זרע למינהו ועץ עשה פרי אשר זרעו
בו למינהו וירא אלהים כי טוב ויהי
ערב ויהי בקר יום שלישי
ויאמר אלהים יהי מארת ברקיע
השמים להבדיל בין היום ובין
הלילה והיו לאתת ולמועדים ולימים
ושנים והיו למאורת ברקיע השמים
להאיר על הארץ ויהי כן ויעש

עליה ג׳

9. וַיֹּ֣אמֶר אֱלֹהִ֗ים יִקָּו֨וּ הַמַּ֜יִם
מִתַּ֤חַת הַשָּׁמַ֙יִם֙ אֶל־מָק֣וֹם אֶחָ֔ד
וְתֵרָאֶ֖ה הַיַּבָּשָׁ֑ה
וַֽיְהִי־כֵֽן׃

10. וַיִּקְרָ֨א אֱלֹהִ֤ים ׀ לַיַּבָּשָׁה֙ אֶ֔רֶץ
וּלְמִקְוֵ֥ה הַמַּ֖יִם קָרָ֣א יַמִּ֑ים
וַיַּ֥רְא אֱלֹהִ֖ים כִּי־טֽוֹב׃

11. וַיֹּ֣אמֶר אֱלֹהִ֗ים
תַּֽדְשֵׁ֤א הָאָ֙רֶץ֙
דֶּ֔שֶׁא
עֵ֚שֶׂב מַזְרִ֣יעַ זֶ֔רַע
עֵ֣ץ פְּרִ֞י
עֹ֤שֶׂה פְּרִי֙ לְמִינ֔וֹ
אֲשֶׁ֥ר זַרְעוֹ־ב֖וֹ עַל־הָאָ֑רֶץ
וַֽיְהִי־כֵֽן׃

After the Torah reading, recite the following blessing.

בָּרוּךְ אַתָּה יְיָ אֱלֹהֵינוּ מֶלֶךְ הָעוֹלָם, אֲשֶׁר נָתַן לָנוּ תּוֹרַת אֱמֶת,
וְחַיֵּי עוֹלָם נָטַע בְּתוֹכֵנוּ. בָּרוּךְ אַתָּה יְיָ, נוֹתֵן הַתּוֹרָה.

We praise You, Adonai our God, Ruler of the universe,
Who planted eternal life among us by giving us a Teaching of truth.

We praise You, Adonai, the Giver of Torah.

TA'AMEI HA-MIKRA: TROP CHARTS

Let's face it: learning trop can be very difficult. Most of us are used to the idea that each musical sign represents a single tone, but with trop, most signs (*ta'amim*) represent musical phrases. To add to the difficulty, there are 28 separate trop signs — each with a unique musical phrase, and sometimes the phrasing changes depending on the combination of *ta'amim* (though very few readings contain all 28 *ta'amim*). Sure, you can find sheet music to help you out, but if you're like me and don't read music, you might wind up more confused. Oy!

I developed the charts in this section to help people like me. Most of the *ta'amim* are grouped into sequences that are used commonly in the Tana<u>h</u>. The grids enable the teacher and the student to chart the music as it goes higher or lower.

These charts have proven quite helpful with my own students. I hope you find them just as useful!

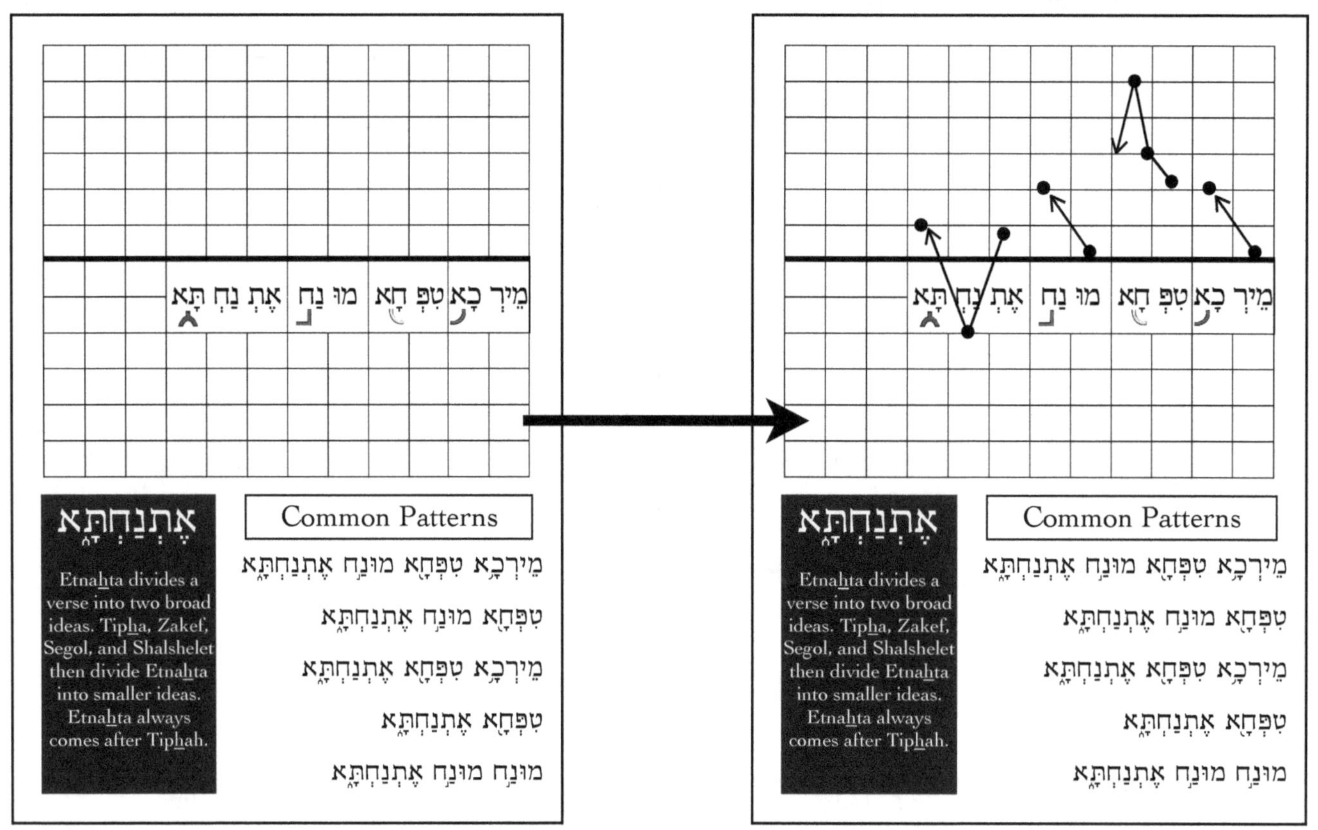

What's the point of all this trop?

Apart from musical notations, the trop (or, more properly, *te'amim*) tell us where to put the correct emphasis in each word and sentence. They also function as grammatical and syntactical notations, telling us when to pause in our reading, when to read quickly, etc. So we don't just read the punctuation — we sing it! There are seven distinct vocal systems for chanting the Tana<u>h</u>. Most people are familiar with Torah and Haftarah. See if you can find out what the other five are!

TORAH TROP

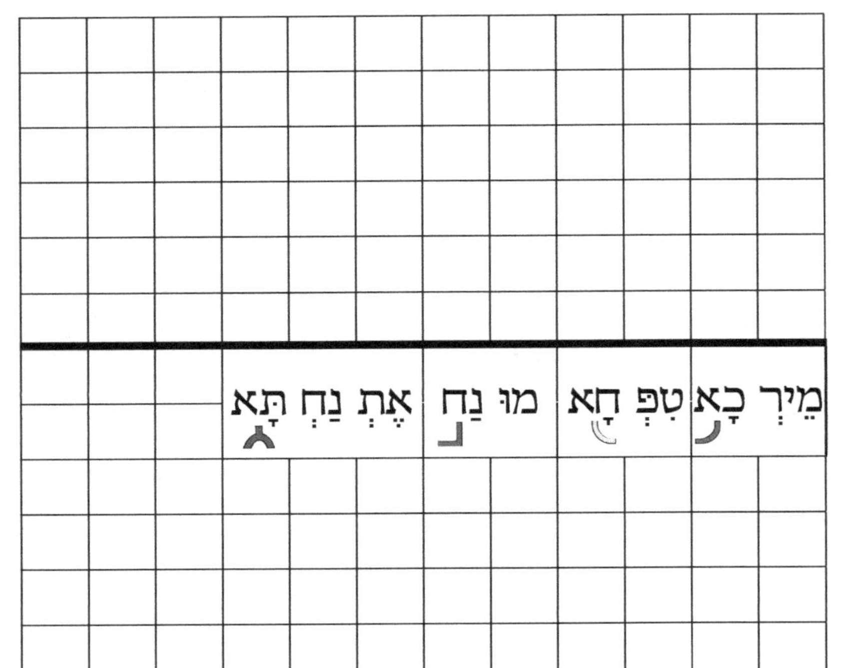

אֶתְנַחְתָּא

Etna<u>h</u>ta divides a verse into two broad ideas. Tip<u>h</u>a, Zakef, Segol, and Shalshelet then divide Etna<u>h</u>ta into smaller ideas. Etna<u>h</u>ta always comes after Tip<u>h</u>ah.

Common Patterns

מֵירְכָא טִפְחָא מוּנַח אֶתְנַחְתָּא

טִפְחָא מוּנַח אֶתְנַחְתָּא

מֵירְכָא טִפְחָא אֶתְנַחְתָּא

טִפְחָא אֶתְנַחְתָּא

מוּנַח מוּנַח אֶתְנַחְתָּא

מֵירְ כָא טִפְ חָא מֵירְ כָא סוֹף פָּ סוּק

סוֹף-פָּסוּק

Sof Pasuk is also called סִילוּק (Siluk). It marks the end of a verse. Tip<u>h</u>a and Zakef subdivide Sof Pasuk into smaller ideas. Sof Pasuk always comes after Tip<u>h</u>ah.

Common Patterns

מֵירְכָא טִפְחָא

מֵירְכָא סוֹף-פָּסוּק

טִפְחָא מֵירְכָא סוֹף-פָּסוּק

מֵירְכָא טִפְחָא סוֹף-פָּסוּק

טִפְחָא סוֹף-פָּסוּק

TORAH TROP

קָ טּ֒וֹן מַהְ פַּ֤ךְ פַּשְׁ טָא֙ מוּ נַ֣ח קָ טּ֒וֹן

זָקֵף־קָט֔וֹן

Zakef divides Etna<u>h</u>ta and Sof Pasuk into smaller ideas, but only if they already have a Tip<u>h</u>a. Revi'a, Pashta and Yetiv suubdivide Zakef into even simpler ideas. Zakef-Katon (a.k.a Katon) is more common than Zakef-Gadol.

Common Patterns

מוּנַ֣ח קָט֔וֹן

מַהְפַּ֤ךְ פַּשְׁטָא֙ מוּנַ֣ח קָט֔וֹן

פַּשְׁטָא֙ קָט֔וֹן

יְ֚תִיב קָט֔וֹן
(see Yetiv card)

יְ֚תִיב מוּנַ֣ח קָט֔וֹן
(see Yetiv card)

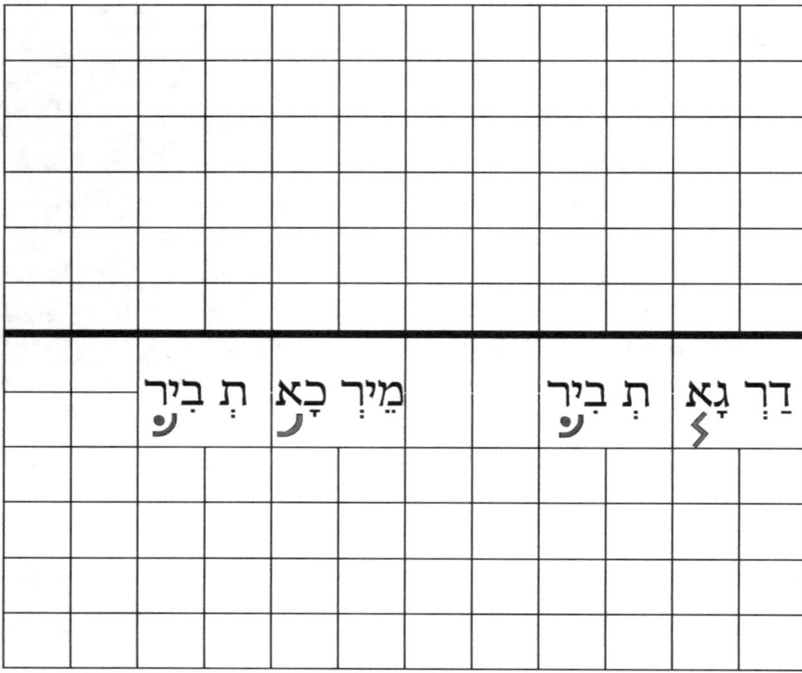

תְּבִ֛יר

When a Tip<u>h</u>a idea has three or more words, it needs to be subdivided. We use Tevir for this subdivision.

Common Patterns

דַּרְגָּ֧א תְּבִ֛יר

מֵירְכָ֥א תְּבִ֛יר

קַדְמָ֨א מֵירְכָ֥א תְּבִ֛יר

מוּנַ֣ח דַּרְגָּ֧א תְּבִ֛יר

מוּנַ֣ח מֵירְכָ֥א תְּבִ֛יר

TORAH TROP

סֶגוֹל

Segol divides Etnahta into smaller ideas, but only if it already has a Tipha and at least one Zakef. Revi'a, Pashta, Yetiv, and Zarka subdivide Segol into simpler ideas. Segol never appears on the first word of a verse.

Common Patterns

מוּנַח סֶגוֹל

מוּנַח זַרְקָא מוּנַח סֶגוֹל

זַרְקָא סֶגוֹל

זָ קֵף גָּ דוֹל

זָקֵף־גָּדוֹל

Zakef divides Etnahta and Sof Pasuk into smaller ideas, but only if they already have a Tipha. Revi'a, Pashta and Yetiv suubdivide Zakef into even simpler ideas. Zakef-Gadol is only found on short words and it never uses a Link.

Common Patterns

זָקֵף-גָּדוֹל

TORAH TROP

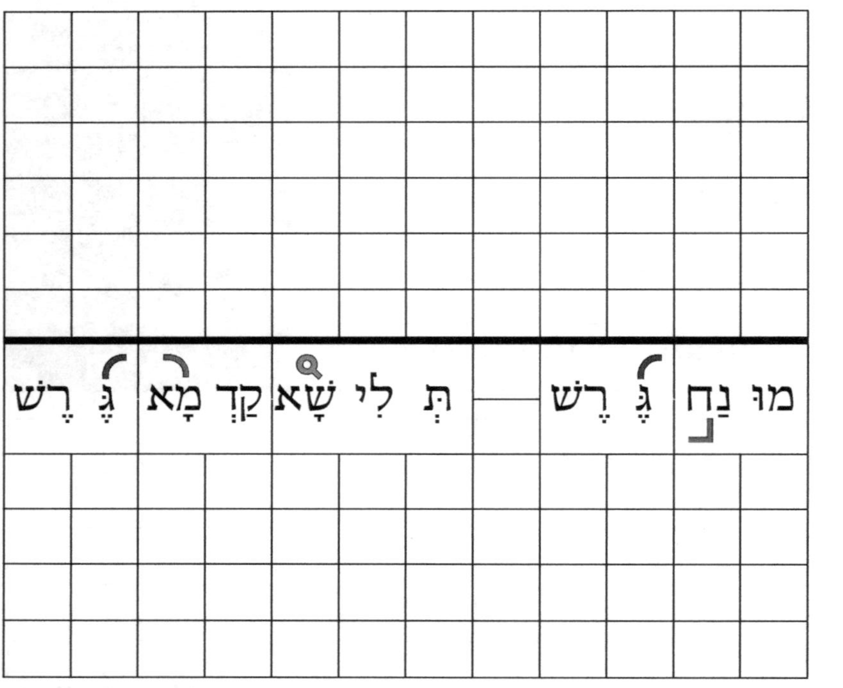

גֵּרֶשׁ

If a Tevir, Pashta, Revi'a or Zarka needs to be subdivided, the subdivider is usually Geresh or Gershayim.

Common Patterns

גֵּ֜רֶשׁ

קַדְמָ֨א גֵּ֜רֶשׁ
(a.k.a. קַדְמָ֨א וְאַזְלָ֜א)

קַדְמָ֨א גֵּ֜רֶשׁ

תְּלִישָׁא-קְטַנָּה קַדְמָא גֵּ֜רֶשׁ

מוּנַח גֵּ֜רֶשׁ

רְ בִי עַ — לְ גַרְ מֵהּ | מוּ נַח רְ בִי עַ

רְבִיעַ

When Tip<u>h</u>a, Zakef, or Segol need to be subdivided and they have one or two Tevirs, Revi'a is used as the Divider.

Common Patterns

רְבִ֗יעַ

מוּנַ֣ח רְבִ֗יעַ

לְגַרְמֵ֣הּ | מוּנַ֣ח רְבִ֗יעַ

TORAH TROP

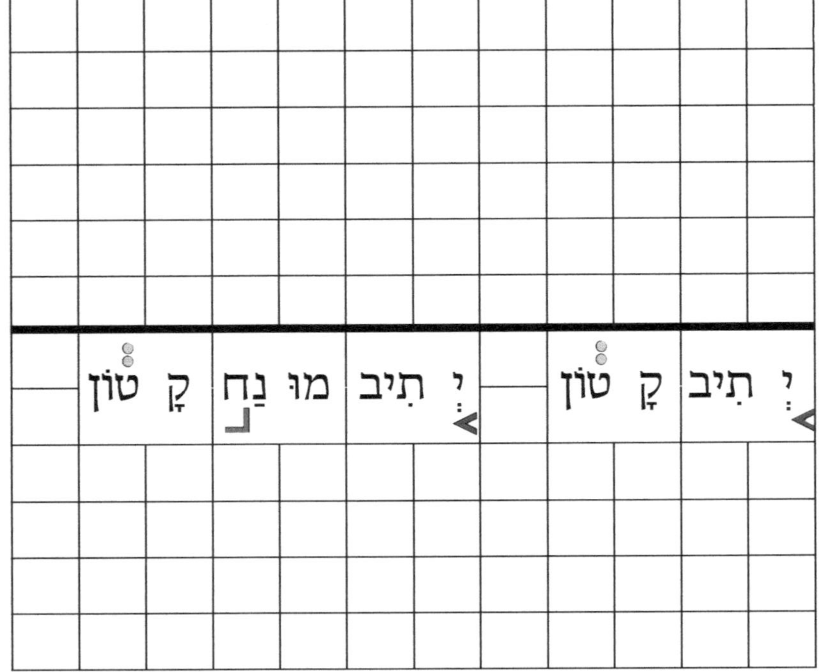

Common Patterns

יְתִיב

יְתִיב קָטֹון

יְתִיב מוּנַח קָטֹון

יְתִיב פַּשְׁטָא
(rare)

יְתִיב

Pashta is only used on the last or second-last syllable of a word. If a Pashta is needed on the first syllable, we use Yetiv, instead. Yetiv never uses a Link.

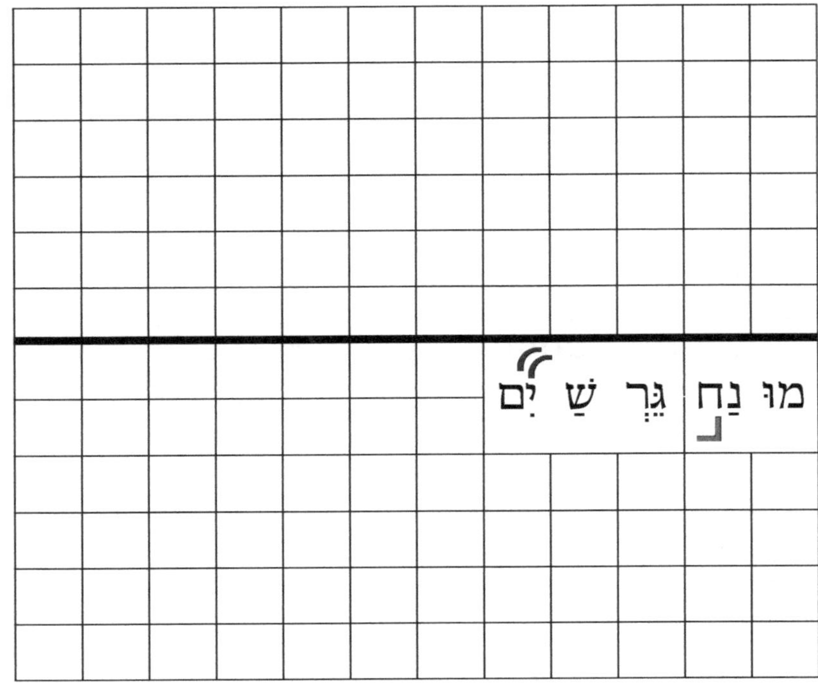

Common Patterns

גֵּרְשַׁיִם

מוּנַח גֵּרְשַׁיִם

גֵּרְשַׁיִם

If a Tevir, Pashta, Revi'a or Zarka needs to be subdivided, the subdivider is usually Geresh or Gershayim.

Torah Trop

מוּ נַח תְּ לִי שָׁא

תְּלִישָׁא-גְדוֹלָה

When Tevir, Revi'a, Pashta, or Zarka need to be subdivided, Telishah-Gedolah is sometimes used. When the accent is not on the first syllable, a second Telishah-Gedolah is often added to mark the stress. Telishah-Gedolah can be linked to up to six Munahs.

Common Patterns

מוּנַח תְּלִישָׁא-גְדוֹלָה

מוּ נַח פָּ זֵר

פָּזֵר

Pazer is used to subdivide Tevir, Revi'a, Pashta, and Zarka. Pazer can be linked to up to six Munahs.

Common Patterns

מוּנַח פָּזֵר

D'VAR TORAH WRITING GUIDE

This guide is intended to give you a general idea of what a typical D'var Torah looks like. Yours may not look exactly like this — it will, of course, be written by you and not me! — but it should include all of these elements. As always, make sure you consult with your rabbi / teacher.

1. Don't thank people for coming — that's something you can tell your guests at the party afterwards. The person giving the D'var Torah is called a *Darshan* — literally, an "explainer". The congregation will thank *you* for explaining the weekly readings to *them*.

2. In one or two paragraphs, summarize the content of the Torah and Haftarah readings for that day.

3. Quote a verse or idea from the Torah and/or Haftarah in Hebrew and in English, and discuss its relevance in our times. This is when you bring in your own commentaries and tell us what you've learned from our ancient and modern teachers.

4. Explain how the idea you've chosen has meaning to you. You can discuss the impact the D'var Torah may have had on how you're going to lead your life, how it's affected your commitment to Judaism and its values, etc.

5. If it fits with your ideas, you may want to talk about your parents, grandparents or other family members and role models and what positive values or lessons you've learned from them. Note: this is not the same as thanking them. Save the "thank you's" for after the service!

6. Final thoughts: what does becoming a Bar/Bat Mitzvah mean to you? Why is it special to you and what have you learned in the process of studying for today? Typically, this is where you bring your discussion back to the original idea you chose from the Torah / Haftarah.

7. Your D'var Torah should be no more than four or five double-spaced pages — roughly the length of a five to seven minute speech.

My ***parashah***, book from the Torah, and chapter/verse	
My ***Haftarah*** book and chapter/verse reference...	

What the TORAH **says in my own words:**	**What the** HAFTARAH **says in my own words:**

Questions I have about my TORAH **reading, Haftarah, Bar/Bat Mitzvah process, or Judaism in general (minimum 3):**	**Questions my parents have about my** TORAH **reading, Haftarah, Bar/Bat Mitzvah process, or Judaism in general (minimum 3):**

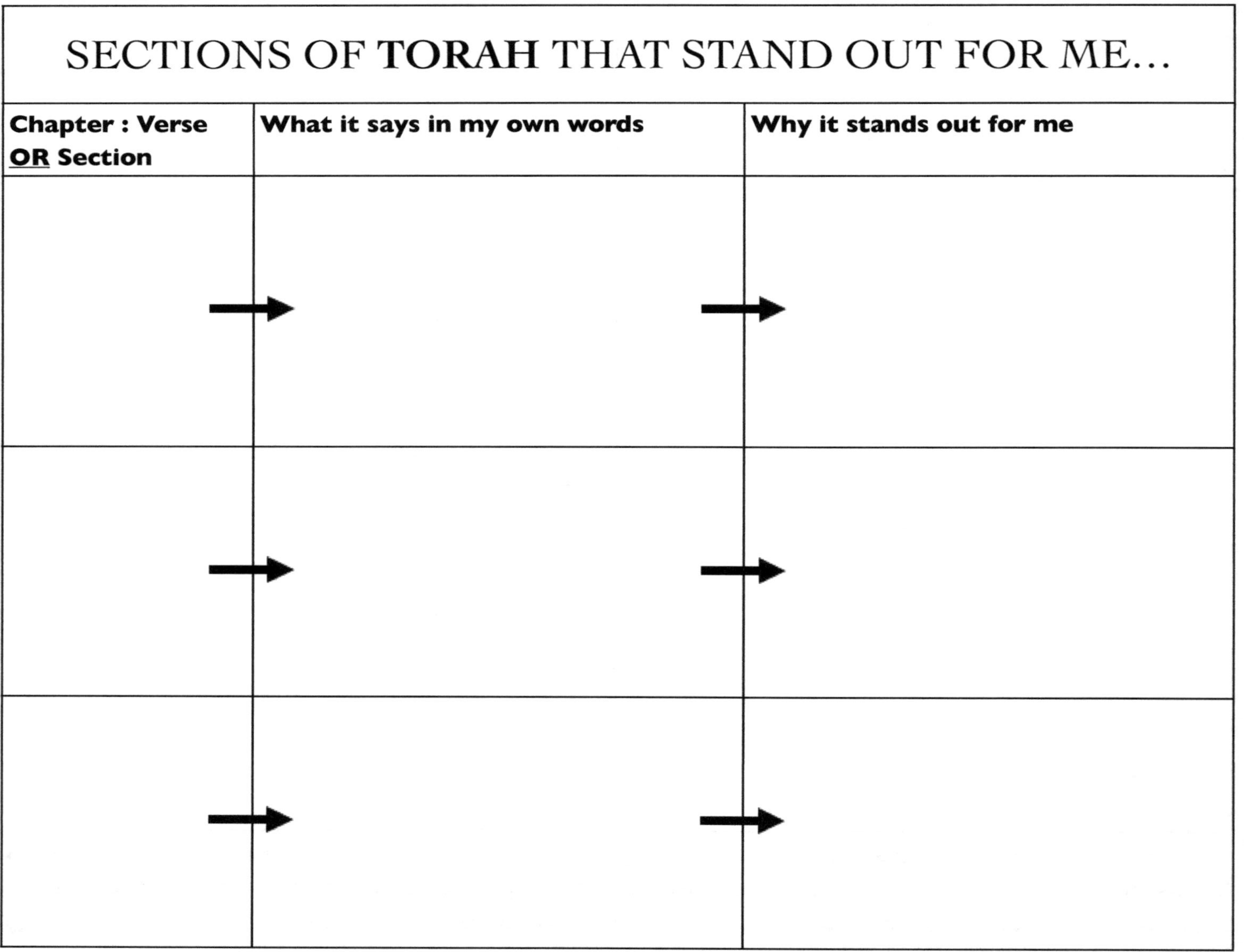

SECTIONS OF **TORAH** THAT STAND OUT FOR ME…

Chapter : Verse OR Section	What it says in my own words	Why it stands out for me

SECTIONS OF **HAFTARAH** THAT STAND OUT FOR ME…		
Chapter : Verse **<u>OR</u> Section**	**What it says in my own words**	**Why it stands out for me**

One idea or theme I want to talk about (based on my choices from charts 3 and 4):	
Verse or section from the Torah or Haftarah that relates to my theme (choose 1 or 2 from charts 3 and/or 4 and write them here):	

Commentator	**The commentator's own words**	**What I think the commentator is trying to teach**
→	→	
→	→	
→	→	

One idea or theme I want to talk about: (copy from previous chart)	
Verse or section from the Torah or Haftarah that relates to my theme: (copy from previous chart)	

Commentator (copy from previous chart)	**What I think the commentator is trying to teach** (copy from previous chart)	**How this teaching relates to my life or the world around me**

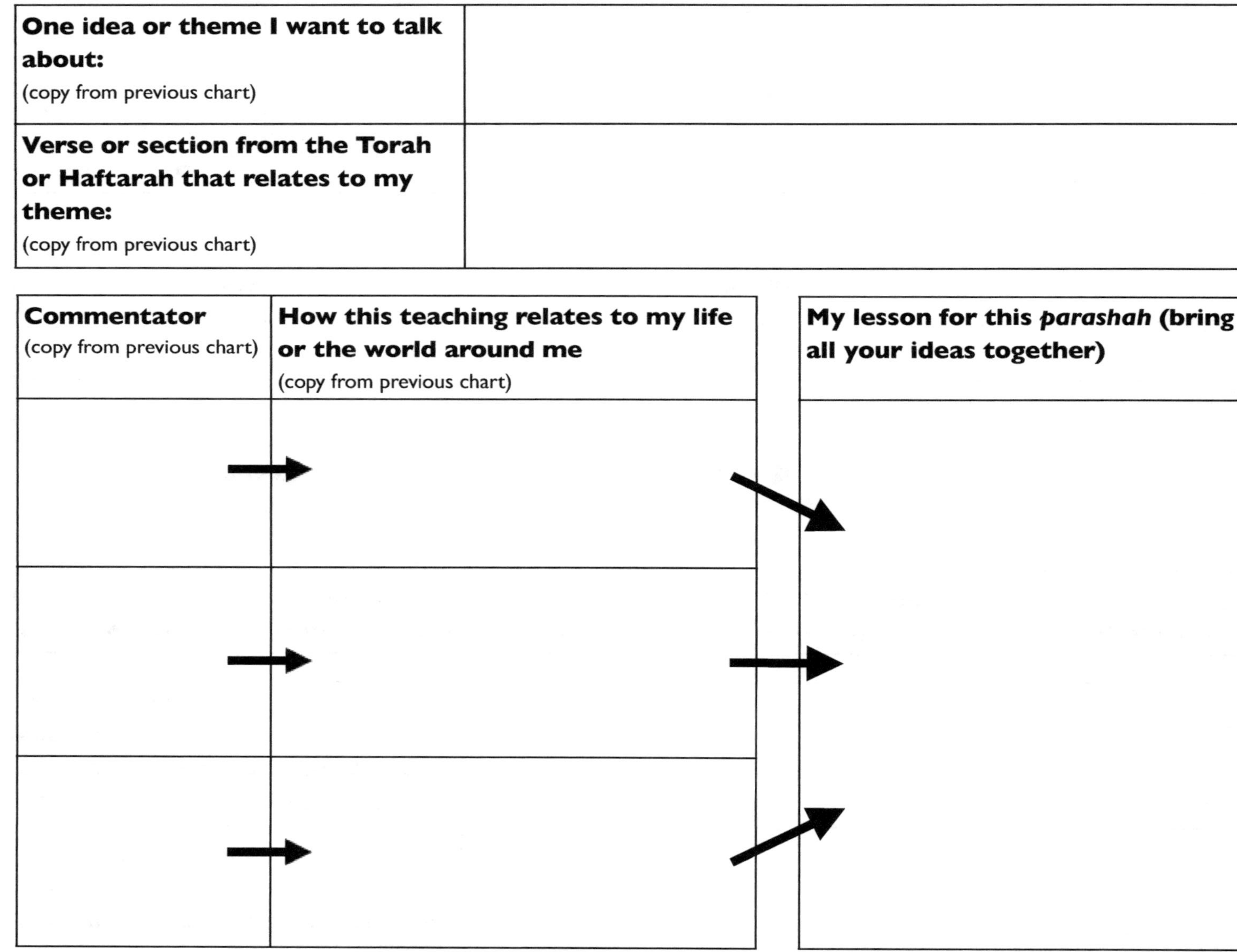

One idea or theme I want to talk about: (copy from previous chart)	
Verse or section from the Torah or Haftarah that relates to my theme: (copy from previous chart)	

Commentator (copy from previous chart)	**How this teaching relates to my life or the world around me** (copy from previous chart)

My lesson for this *parashah* (bring all your ideas together)

INCREDIBLY HANDY TIME LINE

The dates here are approximate. The two main columns compare the Tanah's chronology with samples of writings from ancient Yisra'el's neighbors that relate to events in the Tanah. There are also thousands of Hebrew inscriptions and documents dug up by archeologists, but unfortunately I don't have space to mention them all! The narrow column on the left shows you when the books of the Torah and *Nevi'im* (Prophets) take place, **not** when they were written. See if you can locate your own Torah / Haftarah readings on this time line!

When Torah Books Take Place	Time Line from the Tanah (Torah & Prophets only)		Stuff Written About Yisra'el by Yisra'el's Neighbors
Bereshit	First Jewish family: Avraham, Sarah, Yitzhak, Rivkah, Ya'akov, Le'ah, Rahel, Yosef and all his brothers	1600 BCE 3600 years ago	
	Benay Yisra'el in Mitzra'im	1500 BCE 3500 years ago	
		1400 BCE 3400 years ago	
Shemot, Vayikra, Bamidbar, Devarim		1300 BCE 3300 years ago	
	Time of Moshe and the Exodus	1200 BCE 3200 years ago	Egyptian Pharaoh Merneptah records a list of nations living in Cana'an. "Yisra'el" is included in the list (1205 BCE)
	Benay Yisra'el capture land of Yisra'el		

When *Navi* Books Take Place			
	Benay Yisra'el in Mitzra'im Time of Moshe and the Exodus	1200 BCE 3200 years ago	Egyptian Pharaoh Merneptah records a list of nations living in Cana'an. "Yisra'el" is included in the list (1205 BCE)
Yehoshu'a, Shoftim	Benay Yisra'el capture the land of Yisra'el and settle it. Time of the *Shoftim* (tribal chiefs).	1100 BCE 3100 years ago	
Shemu'el	Time of King Sha'ul, King David and King Shlomo; First Temple is built; Kingdom of Yisra'el established	1000 BCE 3000 years ago	
1 Melahim	Kingdom splits into Yehudah and Yisra'el (922 BCE) Book of *1 Melahim* describes invasion of Yehudah by Pharaoh Shishak	900 BCE 2900 years ago	Egyptian Pharaoh Shishak writes a victory monument about invading the region in and around Yisra'el
2 Melahim Amos, Hoshe'a, Nahum, Micah, Yish'ayah #1	Time of Eliyahu and Elisha; Book of *2 Melahim* describes a rebellion against Yisra'el by Mesha, king of Mo'ab; *2 Melahim* also describes war between Aram, Yehudah, and Yisra'el	800 BCE 2800 years ago	King Mesha of Mo'ab makes a stone monument describing his rebellion against Israel; Anonymous king of Aram makes a stone monument describing war with Yehudah & Yisra'el
	Ashur conquers Yisra'el (722-720 BCE) Books of *2 Melahim* and *Yish'ayah* describe Assyrian invasions of Yehudah and Yisra'el	700 BCE 2700 years ago	Assyrian kings Tiglath-Pileser III and Shalmaneser V write inscriptions and wall carvings about conquering Israel; Assyrian king Sennacherib writes inscription about his invasion of Yehudah
2 Melahim Tzefanyah, Yirmiyah, Yehezk'el, Yish'ayah #2, Ovadyah	**Bavel conquers Yehudah (590's-586 BCE)** Yerushalayim destroyed (586 BCE)	600 BCE 2600 years ago	**Babylonians write inscriptions about their invasion and conquest of Yehudah**
Hagai, Zeharyah, Habakuk, Mal'ahi	Cyrus of Persia allows exiles to return from Bavel; Temple rebuilt; time of Nehemiyah & Ezra	500 BCE 2500 years ago	Persia conquers Babylon; Persian King Cyrus II writes inscription about his policy of allowing all exiled people to return home

When Navi books take place	Events		Date	Events	
When *Navi* Books Take Place	Cyrus of Persia allows exiles to return from Bavel; Temple rebuilt; time of Nehemiyah & Ezra		500 BCE 2500 years ago	Persia conquers Babylon; Persian King Cyrus II writes inscription about his policy of allowing all exiled people to return home	
Hagai, Zeharyah, Habakuk, Mal'ahi			400 BCE 2400 years ago		
		Books of the Torah, Prophets, and other pieces of literature are edited and compiled into the Tanah	300 BCE 2300 years ago	Greek Empire defeats Persia and takes control of the land of Israel	
		Jews successfully rebel against Greek Seleucid Empire & establish kingdom of Judea (Hanukah)	200 BCE 2200 years ago		
	Time of the Mishnah (final compilation roughly 200 CE)		100 BCE 2100 years ago	Dead Sea Scrolls are written and hidden in caves in the Judean Desert	Roman Empire takes control of Judea
		Jews rebel against Rome; Jerusalem and the Temple are destroyed (70 CE)	1 BCE / 1 CE 2000 years ago		**Romans build a massive arch with carvings that depict the victory over the Jews**
			200 CE 1800 years ago		

Ease your way into learning the Trop for Torah and Haftarah!

Our Trop Flashcards enhance any Bar/Bat Mitzvah study program. 28 5"x7" flashcards feature:

- the position of each ta'am in a word
- explanations that let you know what each ta'am is used for
- the most common patterns for each ta'am
- handy music charts
- a color-coding system to help students visualize the music
- suggestions for use
- terribly convenient explanatory notes and charts

Each set also includes a 12-page booklet that explains how the Trop system works.

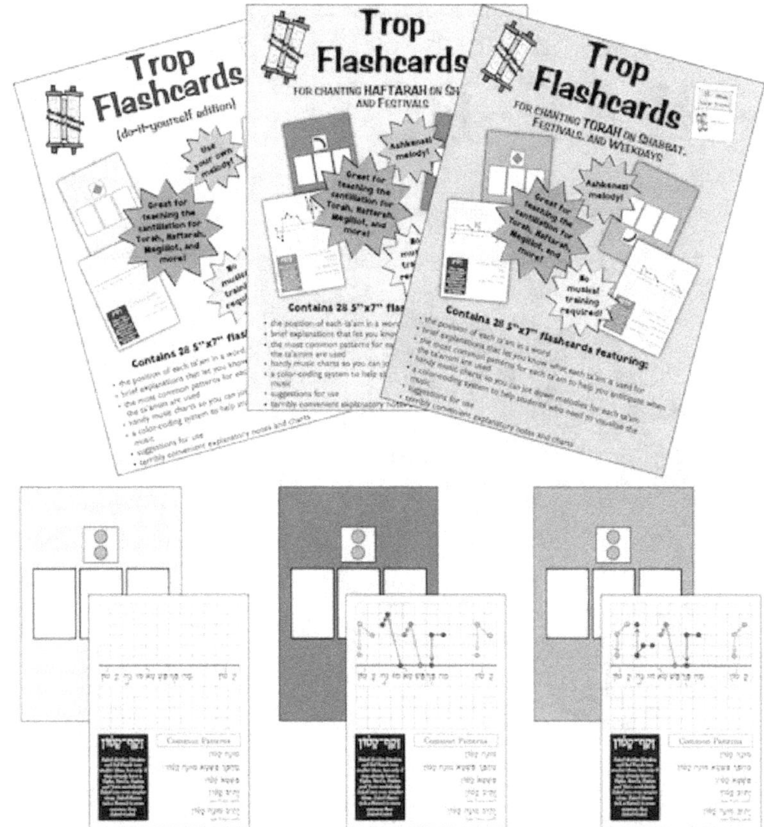

Zakef-Katon card, Do-It-Yourself edition (front and back sides).

Zakef-Katon card, Haftarah edition (front and back sides).

Zakef-Katon card, Torah edition (front and back sides).

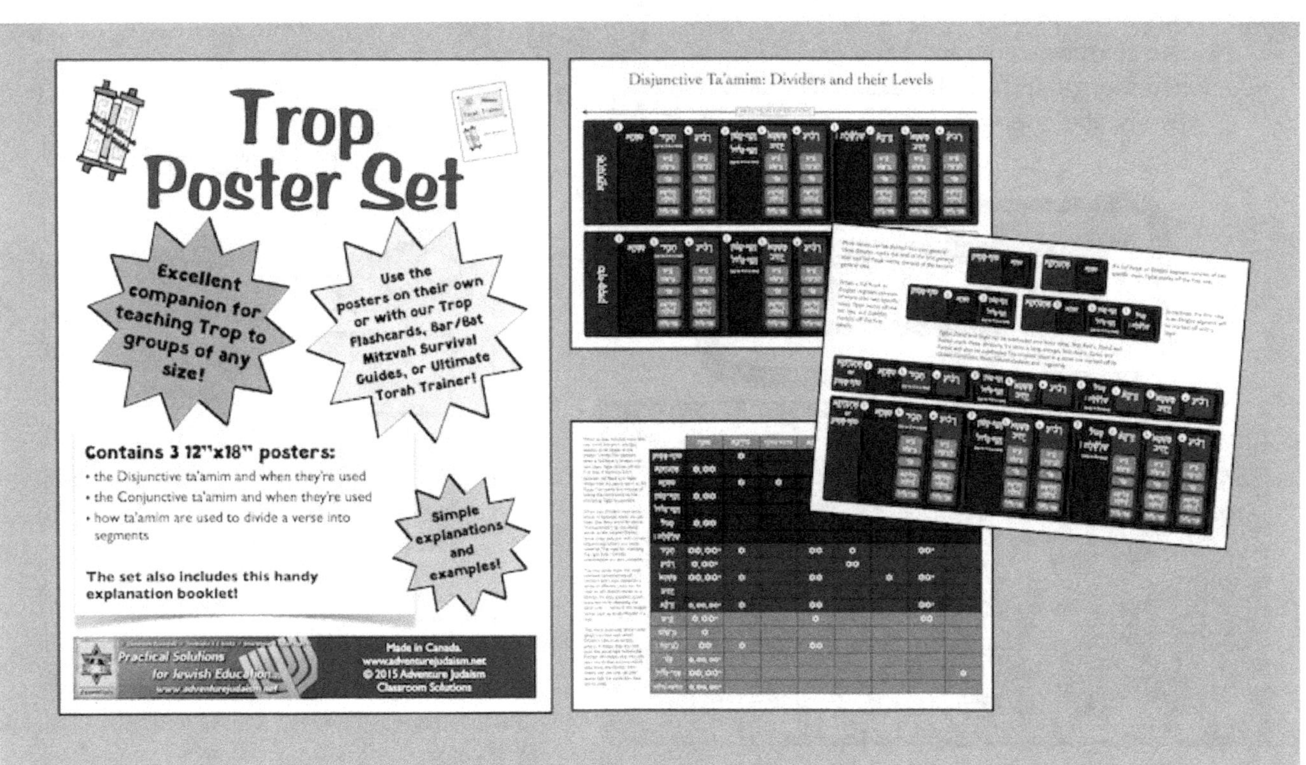

www.adventurejudaism.net

www.adventurejudaism.net

A fun way to learn about the Holy Days and the order of the Hebrew months!

The Hebrew months and Holy Days come alive with the Hagim & Hodashim Cards series. Meet any classroom or programming need with our large display cards, flashcards for small groups, or playing cards for active learning through games. Use them for:

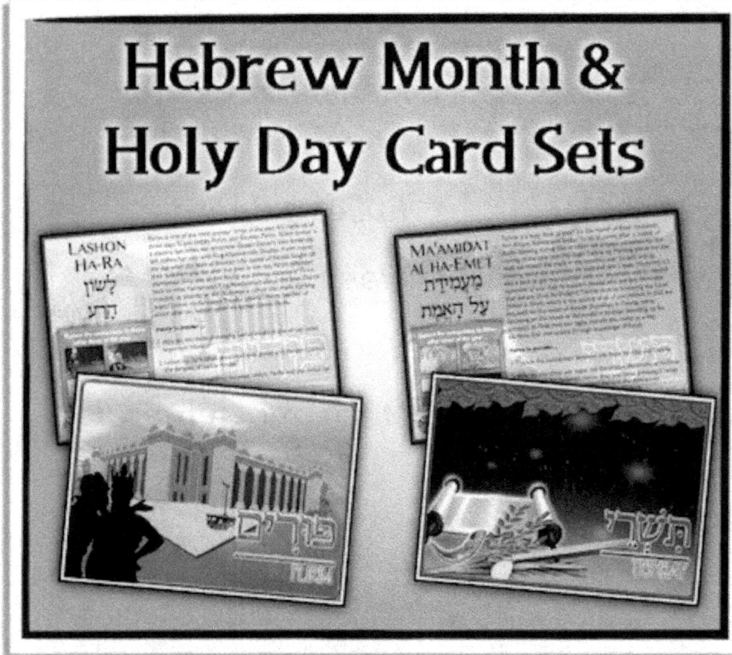

- *Learning the order of the Hebrew months and Holy Days*
- *Connecting months and events inthe year to Jewish values*
- *Designing a values-based program for the year*
- *And more!*

The 11"x8" display cards are perfect for word walls, sorting games, class displays, and more.

The 7"x5" flashcards are great for working with small groups.

The 4"x3" playing cards are great for match games, fish, memory games, and more. Suggestions for games are included.

www.adventurejudaism.net

www.ingramcontent.com/pod-product-compliance
Lightning Source LLC
LaVergne TN
LVHW081423110826
845149LV00010B/1854

* 9 7 8 0 9 8 7 7 8 0 9 2 8 *